INDIA - UNBOUND UNHINGED

SOMITRA VARDHAN DUBEY

Made with ♥ on the Notion Press Platform
www.notionpress.com

For the youth of India, the inheritors of our nation's legacy, the architects of its future. May these poems spark dialogue, ignite passion, and inspire action. For those who grapple with the complexities of our democracy, who seek truth amidst the noise, and who strive for a better India. May these verses offer reflection, provoke thought, and encourage constructive engagement.For the restless hearts of India, seeking truth in the tapestry of our nation, may these verses resonate with the rhythm of your hopes and struggles.For a India where caste is no barrier, where women rise to their full potential, and where every voice is heard.

The initiation of the idea was from my mother Smt Sonali Dubey irrespective of her own personal thoughts.

Contents

Preface — vii

Acknowledgements — ix

1. U C UCC! — 1

2. INDO CHINA — 2

3. AYYEEE WOMANIYA — 4

4. CASTING THE CASTE — 6

5. RUSSIA-UKRAINE X INDIAN EYES — 8

6. GUILEFUL GUJJUS — 10

7. INDO PAK — 12

8. PALESTINE X INDIAN EYES — 14

9. MERA MADHYA PRADESH — 16

10. INDIAN POLITICS — 18

11. Haunting Vallabh Bhawan — 21

12. Hindi Hits — 23

13. AAYIEN NA HUMARE... — 25

14. OPPOSITION? — 26

15. AHEM AHEM YOU THERE? — 27

16. SAR — 29

17. KHULLE AAM? — 30

18. HINDI HITS #2 — 32

19. N(JACK) — 33

Preface

This collection of poems comes straight from the heart – a heart deeply connected to India. It's a land of crazy contradictions, where ancient traditions bump up against modern life, stunning landscapes sit next to real social problems, and the past is always whispering in the present's ear. These poems are my way of trying to capture all that, to explore the different experiences that make up being Indian, and to give a voice to the stories that often get missed.

India's politics, with its messy mix of ideas, power plays, and social movements, is a big part of what these poems are about. From the big national stories to what's happening in local neighborhoods, politics is everywhere. I haven't shied away from the tough stuff – corruption, injustice, the fight for everyone to have a fair say. I'm not trying to give easy answers, but I do hope these poems get people thinking, talking, and understanding a bit more about what makes our society tick.

A big focus here is on the lives of women in India. In a society where things are often stacked against them, women show incredible strength and resilience. These poems are about celebrating that, about giving voice to their experiences – from facing violence and discrimination to achieving amazing things. You can't tell the real story of India without talking about the struggles and triumphs of its women.

And then there's the whole issue of caste, which is still a huge problem. These poems try to shine a light on the unfairness of it all, to give voice to those who've been pushed to the margins for generations. It's a call for justice, for equality, for a future where your caste doesn't decide your destiny. India can't truly move forward until everyone, regardless of caste, can live with dignity.

These poems aren't just me observing from a distance; they're me trying to get inside the heart of India, to feel its heartbeat, and connect with what makes us all human. I believe that what happens to us personally is connected to what's happening in the world around us. These poems explore that connection, showing how big social forces affect individual lives, and giving voice to the hopes, fears, and dreams of everyday Indians.

I really hope these poems connect with you, get you thinking, and maybe even spark some conversations. Ultimately, this collection is about the power of poetry to show the complexities of life, bridge divides, and inspire us to build a fairer India for everyone. It's for everyone who's working towards a better tomorrow, where everyone gets a voice and everyone is valued.

Acknowledgements

"The completion of this work would not have been possible without the invaluable assistance of several individuals. I extend my sincerest gratitude to my parents ,elder brother, whose insightful guidance and unwavering support were instrumental in shaping this project.

I am deeply indebted to my teachers and various news sources for their academic contribution. Their contributions have significantly enhanced the quality of this work.

I would also like to acknowledge the support of Gemini by Google and Grammarly for refinig and fine tuning the manuscript.

Finally, I express my sincere appreciation to Notion. Their dedication and expertise have been invaluable in bringing this book to fruition."

ACKNOWLEDGEMENTS

The author and his mother

1. U C UCC!

This is a cloth woven, threads of various shades,
Crimson, saffron, green, white, and blue.
Each thread a custom, a faith, a way of life,
Woven together in harmony and strife.
Some look for pattern, one continuous thread,
Uniform doctrine, from toe to head.
In common are mentioned equality, justice for all,
Old divisions lose their spell.
But fear for the shearing of their thread strikes others:
The extinction of a tradition, the words of their fathers.
They relish the nuances, the subtle design,
Woven through ages, a heritage divine.
The cloth wavered, as tensions grew,
Sum unity calls and ancestral ties.
In one thread, is it possible to leave such expanse to bind?
Or shall it rather go asunder the roots of days gone by?
This question has remained for long, deep and unanswered:
How to honor diversity, while the promise shall keep,
When there is talk about fairness and justice for all,
In this obliterated tapestry, finding its place.
Your thoughts

2. INDO CHINA

The pride of India, a place of Sadhu living
Where empires rise, and empires fall with guile and stubborn
striving.
From ancient times, through silk roads and modern trade,
An entangled history; in this turbulent space.
A thorn itself, in the side of India, is Aksai Chin,
Claimed for her glory in the skies of China.
Perched are Ladakh's icy peaks, where the clash between patrols
unfolds,
As tensions unravel.
1962 reigned in September, showing you bitter, haunting stings,
The wound just begins to bleed, the settled memory shall not
cease to sing.
A bloody and brutal engagement in Galwan Valley,
Where soldiers fell in the cold, harsh, and unyielding way.
Shadows dance beyond the border, a power-play;
A tussle at the economic front, with fortunes ebbing their flow.
The Belt and Road is a snake quandary, rapidly unfurling,
India's caution rising as tides favor its influence.
The specter of war, a constant, chilling dread,
A nuclear shadow hovering overhead.
Ineffective dances through diplomatic ties,

As trust is eroded, so too rises tension.
A search for peace does demand an uphill-like strive,
But a wade far more infested and full of all knotted brambles
should be put to the test.
But, oh hope: a spark for the cool night.
A dialogue whereby reason could bring forth the light.
Your thoughts

3. AYYEEE WOMANIYA

In Bharat's tapestry, women are forced to be laborers and seekers.
However, representation remains as distant and elusive as a May
bee.
Meetings of panchayats or assemblies for decision-making,
It is a male-dominated space-a tired story oftentimes.
The Constitution promises equity,
But society aptly seizes their views and use.
Patriarchy's menace is a nasty little thing,
With their walls representing light, incalculably our woman is
quenched.
Reservations will serve as a corrective step,
An endeavor to break this partly-glass roof, testing their voices.
The Panchayati Raj could serve as that crucible, as a case in
point,
To empower women to rest in their own rightful place.
The opponents say it will dilute the thin beam of merit,
While history tells stories of institutionalized shame.
Centuries-old discrimination, and denied opportunity,
Which ram it through becomes virtually unexamined for
women.

This is not charity, but the question of justice,
To harness their talents, to make their voice count.
It is a nation where pluralism has a say,
And women's leadership has a chance to live again.
The future looks grim, with heart-stopping challenges,
Yet change is born in the burning forge of determination.
No other way-there is a disempowered nation,
Where women's empowerment will one day breathe.
Your thoughts

4. CASTING THE CASTE

The ghost of caste, a specter from an age long gone,
With a deep stain on the soul where inequality lingers.
Though the laws might say once and for all, as if,
Some age-old wounds continue to pour and bite their way in.
A fragile nation, divided along deep yet invisible lines,
Where opportunities vanish and dreams may never wake.
The marginalized languishing, being deprived of a share in
Education, resources, the sort of future worthy of the name.
Some counter that a census will fan the embers of hate,
Revoke the divisions that held the nation's fate.
Data be cast as a weapon to fuel the fires of strife,
Might deepen the abyss of Indian life.
Others also contend that knowledge is power,
Thus equipping them to understand the plight of this hour.
To gauge how deep that social divide can go,
And guide any programs directed where the need doth flow.
To ensure that all people receive inclusion,
To edify the free-spirits that might otherwise have been oppressed.
To build a nation that serves only these truths -- not incongruous
fables,

Where justice reigns, belonging to no fewer, nor yet few.
The road ahead is full of unmitigated terrors and doubts,
Finding a way toward balance while seeking the truth.
To gather data in the most sensitive manner,
To give healing to the wounds of that dark history.
A living nation where uniformity has never been imposed,
But, rather, diversity has always been embraced.
Where, on account of their caste, no one is defined by their
mortality,
But where, rather, their journey is determined by the merit and
talent.
Your thoughts

5. RUSSIA-UKRAINE x INDIAN EYES

The inferno ravenously devours Donbas in alignment,
As shadows grow taller, entangled by the bedrock of doom.
A grand wrestling match, where elephants collide,
And nations ruefully watch from a distant space.
The West condemns, adding sanction with swift force,
Except murmurs, of bananas from ominous banalities.
Arms dealers reap, as arms freely have their heyday,
Death, day by day=innocent, at this price paid.
India cautiously keeps its eye open,
Sailing currents, painful skies come falling.
A slight balance between east and west,
Finding a way to unfurl, honest and true.
Spread out across the pandemic glance,
Notes such as these always remind that through suffering, pain
hath came.
A pleading for peace, uttered with moaning agony and anguish,
Observed human tears as the world looked down.
Though India recalls intertwined history,
An embrace from Russia-an altered friendship.
Shared struggles, and a common cause,

Space exploration, and scientific adoration.
But here, the fine line, created by net neutrality,
Under such global pretense.
The search for energy, a mantra repeated,
While geopolitical storms work down and again.
A human toll terribly steep,
Beating back refugees-to whom and towards what lands
themselves.
Whether darkened, it appears, in poetry-combatting the blows of
the insane,
Softly dominions, where peace faces and problems arise.
Your thoughts

6. GUILEFUL GUJJUS

*The two behemoths still boom-they are big and will be there for
long,*
The signal, the postmaster, the authors of this great power.
Theirs is a continuum, their imprints in ports and power,
The history of a history against a grand southwest region.
But whispers get to talk about deals at night,
Crony capitalism, and a blinding light.
Regulatory lacquer failings-loopholes so wide,
Where every rule bends, and every fetter loosens up.
The common man is apprehensive;
resources rotting away at the will of mind-blowing cold.
The cost appears to be heavy on the environment,
Like forests taken down, including those rivers, black.
Tax havens, beckoning so rich from within,
While forth are the public coffers empty and cold.
The widening of the gap between the rich and the poor,
By inequality-first it blooms, then slowly rots.
The voice of dissent, from barely a murmur, has grown strong,
*War on the mighty, seeking, with accountability, that which is
supposed to belong.*
For many once favored by the dust of glory
Not in pity for so many, but in their deserved share in the glory.

That won't be a critique of the bare and big objective of
ambition,
But will stand with fairness in the Indian shadow.
A level-playing board, the merit awarded back,
As nation-self wealth is shared, come what may.
Your thoughts

7. INDO PAK

The Line of Control casts her scar on the land,
Demanding to preserve history's ghosts.
Forever on a vigil; it drains us of strength.
Politicians posturing; day and night.
Talks of peace with furrowed brow?
In his face, missiles dance more, tensions rise.
Kashmir is the thorn in his side,
Activating the flame where she believes.
Generals boast of such nobility in their weaponry?
Ignoring the plight of the common man.
Farmers toil on war-scorched land
While the budgets swell for this farce;
The media screams profusely of threats, fears
of infiltration and phantom careers.
They jingoistically whip up a frenzy,
While the consequences, the commoners bear.
So let the bomb fall and the cannons roar
While politicians posturers continue to demand more.
This peace is so elusive, though.
A fragile flower, crushed by the harsh extreme.
And we, the people, find ourselves at
the heavy price for such a fine display.

Of jingoism and political greed
While the dreams for better futures, indeed,
Are shattered by bombs, silenced by fear,
Year in, year out, and year after year.
Your thoughts

8. PALESTINE x INDIAN EYES

In Palestine's cradle, where prophets walked,
There sounds that of conflict, a never ceasing, grim god.
The land has been a battleground, for many decades,
Where narratives collide, and stories wither away.
From Gaza's siege, to settlement woes,
The round of violence that never ceases to be.
The world looks on in pathetically circumspect refrain,
As politicians posture and profits remain.
India watches remote and unengaged,
Lines of navigation all disparate within these troubled times.
A positive voice unfolding,
Submissions for peace but cries about continuing conflict.
For Kashmir's shadow is an overarching and profound one,
Reflected in this battleground among the two.
That very thirst for release seems a universal cry;
But the path to peace tries hard, yet succeeds not.
The news is all about rockets and bombarding,
Unwittingly destroying lives in many incidents.
The stage is a sad, ill-fated one,
While yet another cycle of violence ignores its own scorn.

Let bombs fall silently and rockets fly in waiting,
While politicians profit from the unending diligent plight.
For peace, it seems, presents itself a far distant dream,
A mirage in the desert, tawdry, and pale.
Your thoughts

9. MERA MADHYA PRADESH

The Shivling gleams, a symbol of might,
But shadows linger, in the fading light.
Allegations swirl, of a system gone awry,
Where cronyism thrives, and transparency dies.
The Vyapam scam, a blot on the state's name,
A chilling reminder, of greed and of shame.
Jobs sold and bought, a mockery of merit,
Leaving a trail of despair, bitter and spirit.
The sand mafia, a scourge on the land,
Ravaging rivers, with an iron hand.
Illegal mining, a rampant, unchecked blight,
While environmental laws, fade into the night.
The tender process, a game of deceit,
Where cronies are favored, a bitter defeat.
Roads crumble, and bridges decay, While public funds vanish,
without a trace.
The farmer toils, on land parched and dry,
While schemes languish, and funds simply fly.
The tribal heartland, forgotten and lost,
As corruption festers, at a tremendous cost.

The people watch, with a cynical gaze, As promises fade, in a
haze of disarray.
The Shivling shines, a symbol of grace,
But corruption's stain, mars its sacred space.
Your thoughts

10. INDIAN POLITICS

A land of color, where traditions sit together.
A traveler walks the path to make the journey a blessing.
polo stands with his dreams in the open sky;
While history's shadows whisper, requests demand reply.
From the markets chattering with life to the darkened quiet
lanes,
His name is spoken-along with the debates and refrains.
A bloodline from a tree, yet born deep in the soil,
But leadership is molded through struggle and toil.
He describes the farmers and laborers, but does he know of their
fight?
The pulse of the earth beats where hope abides.
Amid the spice and tea smells.
Could he bridge this rift? Does he understand?
For a captain must listen to the land's voice
To weave it all together, with a steady hand.
At times, when the heat rages, it'd be quite pompous
To assert that it works when the clock ticks slowly always.
To lead is to feed, foster, mend.
And not see that as an end-a means for their end.
As we cast the future-and the bright stage will bless,
An all-tenuring guide to bar from the wound,

Let the question stay: however far we go.
Will-the shepherd, will he? The part of our show.
In a nation where dreams collide once in a while,
Together we bring forth, the INDIA Alliance, by design,
Saffron, tricolor, and the hues of left,
An inter-stitched arrangement in which air turns unbreathable.
BJP's burning desire, a hullabaloo and bold.
But the shade of other vicious deeds are scandalous and cold.
For whispers of votes, sometimes attached with the price of trust,
From the value of honesty rubbed to dust.
While Congress remembers its previously noted pride,
The honest endeavor of polo to make another stride.
But amid the myriad rifts, the floundering losses,
The unity of voices goes beyond transgressing races.
In Bengal, where the heart beats,
The TMC may be rising, even as trouble works its feet,
A bridge of purpose to bridge the mission carried,
For strength in democracy lies where the voices are laid.
A vision of Aam Aadmi, fresh maps to draw,
Yet scandals and investigations turn towards the sap.
muffler himself would need to try very hard,
As every party holds most tightening of the card.
As for the leaders, sadly afraid yet proud,
The sad echoes of defeat remain like puffs of cloud.
A legacy is found alone to swim,
Against a cheer of current that prepares to grant its rim.
And here's to this election that shows both sides of the coin,

For individual focus shines light on support so elegant.
Your thoughts

11. Haunting Vallabh Bhawan

Madhya Pradesh is a state of Chaos
Various innocents are jailed for their boss' payoff
There exists a Vallabh Bhawan where all dealings take place
Writ or right only money decides fate
Some officers live proudly with the bride and bribes
Others are whistleblowers who get caught in the crossfire of the
department's gripe
Castist, Chauvinsist, and Narrsisitic all kinds of Secretaries live
For the connected people, no rules are stiff
Transfers happen at the boss' will
Pay the money you win but sadly such details never spill
Having carefully seen the Bhawan I can positively say
Governments may change but nothing changes the bhawan's hay
day
Officers alleged with serious charges hold on to their posts
While some are not even given justice by the courts
For any daring officer departmental enquiry is the penalty
Whilst the bureaucrats shout for bhopal sixty for indore fifty
But Money is also made of paper, a paper that burns
With eventual time everything turns

The stern secretaries are now being remanded for the bribes they
once demanded
What various officers could not do a 52 kg gold brick has done
but 100 Alleged no strict action
like those officers who have 150 crores, their lives will continue
to be fun
Corruption of 100 crores punishment is none
The great Vallabh Bhawan
Where the files in every floor take a turn
Harrasers in face of OSD do the action
Excellent workers are looplined
conclusively officers 0 money managers (won) one.
Your thoughts

12. Hindi Hits

मध्य प्रदेश में अराजकता का साया,
निर्दोष कारावास, दुखदाई छाया।
वल्लभ भवन में, खेल चलता है,
पैसा ही राजा, निर्णय बदलता है
रिश्वत के दलदल में, डूबे अधिकारी,
मुखबिरि दबे, सहते पीड़ाकारी।
जातिवाद, घमंड, रंग-बिरंगे,
जुड़े हुए लोग, मुक्त हैं बंधनों से
बदली मनमाने, सत्ता का खेल,
पैसा देकर, जीतते हैं बड़े-बड़े।
भवन में भ्रष्टाचार, फैला हुआ है,
सरकार बदले, पर कुरीति नहीं जाए।
गंभीर अपराध, पर दंड नहीं मिलता,
न्याय की पुकार, दबी रहती है
विभागीय कार्रवाई, साहसियों का दमन,
भोपाल-इंदौर, लूट का प्रचलन।
पैसा कागज है, जलता है अंत में,
सचिव भी जेल, भुगतते हैं कष्ट।
"बावन कलि सोना," कर दिखाया कमाल,
करोड़ों का घोटाला, "डेढ़ सौ करोड़" का माल,

पर अपराधी मस्त, बिना किसी डर के
वल्लभ भवन में, फाइलें घूमती हैं
उत्पीड़न होता, मनमानी से
अच्छे काम करने वाले, लूप में फसते,
पैसा ही राजा, सब कुछ वही चलता हो

13. AAYIEN NA HUMARE...

The sun rises Saffron, or sometimes it's Green, But the man in the middle remains on the scene. The voters cast ballots in sun and in rain, Yet somehow Nitish takes the oath once again. He hugs the Lotus, then the Lantern he'll grab, Like a patient who's weary of just one rehab. From "Jungle Raj" critic to "Big Brother" friend, His morals are rubber that famously bend. Poor Tejashwi packed up his bags for the throne, Thinking the "Prince" would at last have his own. But Uncle said "Sorry, my conscience awoke," And the promise of power went up in blue smoke.

"I do this for Bihar!" he claims with a tear, While the bridges dissolve and just disappear. The concrete is weak, but the glue on his seat? Is the strongest invention on any paved street.

The Sultanganj pillars crash down to the wave, A visual metaphor no one can save. But while the state crumbles and falls to the floor, The CM is knocking on the Governor's door.

He's the record-book champ of the swearing-in rite, Changing his jersey in the dead of the night. Democracy's joke is a singular thing: The Court has many jesters, but only one King.

14. OPPOSITION?

The new dome is mighty, the carpets are grand, But a heavy silence descends on the land. The benches sit vacant, the aisles are bare, With no one left seated to question or care.

A hundred forty voices were thrown from the door, Their right to dissent is not safe anymore. The laws are passed quickly, with no one to fight, Like thieves stealing justice in the dead of the night.

The criminal codes changed while the critics were gone, A new era of power has quietly dawned. When the check is removed, and the balance is dead, The crown rests too heavy on one single head.

Divided and broken, they fight for a name, While losing the rules of the democratic game. A captainless army, a fleet without sail, Against such a current, they are destined to fail.

The media watches with a blindfolded eye, Turning truth to a whisper and truth to a lie. To question the leader is treason, they say, In a house where the shadows have conquered the day.

We need the dissenter to hold up the shield, To ensure that the powerful forced are to yield. For a government unchecked by a rival's strong speech, Will put freedom forever out of our reach

15. AHEM AHEM YOU THERE?

After fifteen long winters, the Hand found its grip, But the Captain and Raja let the victory slip. The "Maharaj" worked hard, wiped the sweat from his face, But they gave the high chair to the oldest in the race.

"If promises break, I'll hit the road!" Scindia cried, Kamal Nath smirked with his arrogant pride. "Toh sadak par utar jao," he dared with a sneer, Not knowing that "sadak" would end his career.

In the middle of Holi, the colours turned pale, As twenty-two MLAs set off on a trail. From Bhopal to Bengaluru, the charter planes flew, Leaving Diggy and Nath without a substantial clue. The resort was locked down, the phones were all dead, While the Congress was panic-stricken, clutching its head. The floor test arrived, the numbers were low, And the "Old Fox" of Chhindwara had to pack up and go.

Now Scindia wears Saffron and flies in the sky, As the Civil Aviation (and Telecom) guy. He traded the insults for a Cabinet seat, While the Congress in MP faced a brutal defeat.

They waited for payback in Twenty-Twenty-Three, Thinking "The voter will set the state free." But with Mama's "Laadli" and

Scindia's might, The Hand was extinguished like a blown-out light.

16. SAR

The file moves only if the ego is fed, A "Good Morning, Sir!" is the daily bread. From the peon to the boss in the air-cooled room, If you miss the "Sir," you are destined for doom.
The British left town on a ship long ago, But left us a habit that just will not go. We bow to the chair, to the stamp, to the pen, "Yes Sir, Right Sir, Please Sir, Amen."
You may be a genius with logic so bright, But the Babu decides if your paper is right. "Come back after lunch," is the national song, Where doing things quickly is ethically wrong.
It's not about service, it's not about work, It's the power to pause, the privilege to shirk. In the land of democracy, free and so fair, The King isn't elected; he sits in that chair.

17. KHULLE AAM?

The Lantern was glowing, the exit polls cheered, Then the lights in the counting hall magically disappeared. Tejashwi was winning, the data looked sweet, Till the "Postal Ballots" performed a great feat.

In Hilsa, the margin was twelve little votes, A number so small it got stuck in their throats. The RJD screamed, "Recount the machine!" But the Officer said, "Sir, the slate is now clean."

"Your postal votes are invalid," the Magistrate said, With a smirk on his face and a nod of his head. "The ink is too smudged, or the tick is too light, We're rejecting five hundred to make the math right."

The TV screens froze on the count of the lead, For three hours straight, not a number would bleed. The server was "down," or so we were told, While the dice in the backroom were quietly rolled.

One-ten was the number they gave to the boy, While one-twenty-five was the ruling side's toy. "The certificate's ready!" the winner was hailed, While the guy with the votes found his arguments failed.

They say Munger's result was a violent display, But the real silent violence happened this way. No guns and no lathis, just a pen and a sheet, To ensure that the "Prince" didn't sit in the seat.

"The Sutras are Mutras," the cadres all cried, As they watched their majority get taken for a ride. It's the Bihar Special: A miracle true, Where the loser wins Gold, and the winner gets Blue.

So next time you vote, just remember the trick, It's not who you choose with your finger and click. It's the man with the stamp and the "System" in tow, Who decides in the midnight just who runs the show.

18. HINDI HITS #2

पैदा होते ही नर्स बोली, "लीजिए, आपकी 'पेंशन' आई है," पापा ने
भी चैन की सांस ली, "चलो बुढ़ापे की लाठी पाई है" बचपन तो बस
नाम का था, कंधों पर बस्ता भारी था, खिलौने तो छोटे के लिए थे,
इसके हिस्से तो बस 'ज़िम्मेदारी' थी।

छोटा भाई रमोट तोड़े, तो वो "बच्चा" कहलाता है, तुम ज़रा
आवाज़ ऊंची करो, तो घर सर पे उठाया जाता है "तू बड़ा है,
समझदार बन," ये मंत्र घुट्टी में पिलाया गया, चॉकलेट का बड़ा
टुकड़ा हमेशा, छोटे की प्लेट में ही पाया गया।

दुनिया चाहे मंगल पे जाए, ये 'डेयरी' तक ही जाता है, "धनिया फ्री
मांगना मत भूलना," मां का ये आर्डर आता है लड़की को हाय
बोलने में, इसको पसीने छूटते है, पर आलू-प्याज के भाव तोलने में,
इसके तेवर नही टूटते हैं

बनना था इसको रॉकस्टार, या क्रिकेट के मैदान में जाना था, पर
पिता जी बोले "इंजीनियरिंग कर, हमें समाज को मुँह दिखाना था।"
खुद का फ़ोन टूटा हुआ है, स्क्रीन पर मकड़ी का जाला है, पर बहन
की विदाई के लिए, इसने पी.एफ. (PF) भी तुड़वा डाला है

सैलरी का मैसेज आते ही, इसके चेहरे पर 'सन्नाटा' है, क्योंकि
बिजली, राशन और EMI ने, पहले ही घेरकर डांटा है दोस्तों के
गोवा प्लान पर, ये बस 'हम्म' कह कर टालता है, मिडिल क्लास
का बड़ा बेटा, दरअसल पूरे घर को पालता है

19. N(JACK)

*The pillars of the State must stand alone, To keep the seat of
Justice on its throne. For if the Minister holds the Judge's pen,
The rights of citizens are lost to men.*
*They sought to break the Collegium's quiet seal, With "Eminent
Persons" and a political deal. To place the Executive inside the
room, And weave a web of compromise and gloom.*
*How can the Bench remain truly free, If it owes its debts to the
Powers that be? A Judge who looks to Delhi for his chair, Will
find the spine of Justice stripped and bare.*
*The "Basic Structure" is the final shield, A sacred ground that
simply cannot yield. To let the Cabinet decide the Court's design,
Is to erase the Constitution's boldest line.*
*When a Citizen stands against the State's might, Who protects
the candle of his civil right? Not a Judge selected by the State's
decree, But one who owes his oath to Liberty.*
*So let the amendment lie in history's dust, To keep the temple
worthy of our trust. The Gavel and the Crown must never blend,
Or else the Rule of Law will meet its end.*